The Judgment of God

Advent and Christmas Devotionals

by Lillie Ammann

Published by:
Lillie's Lovely Little Publishing Company
lillie@lillieammann.com
www.lillieammann.com

Proofreaders:
George Lampe
Pam Lampe

Print ISBN: 978-0-9665912-8-6

A Note from the Author

Each year during Advent and Lent, I follow a Bible reading plan. I journal a short meditation and write a brief prayer on each day's reading. The following year, I publish the devotionals.

This book is being published in 2020 with my personal devotions from Advent 2019. I hope you are blessed by these Scriptures, thoughts, and prayers during this holy season.

Thanks to my friends George and Pam Lampe, fellow parishioners at All Saints Anglican Church in San Antonio, for proofreading.

Profits will be donated to Love for the Least (L4L) to share the compassion of Christ with an unreached world. L4L shares the Good News of the Gospel with the least and unreached by making disciples of Jesus who make disciples (2 Tim 2:2) and by helping to meet the physical needs of the poorest of the poor. To learn more, visit lovefortheleast.org.

May His blessings abound in your time alone with Him.

Lillie Ammann
November 2020

The First Sunday in Advent

The day of the Lord will come like a thief in the night. While people are saying, "There is peace and security," then sudden destruction will come upon them as labor pains come upon a pregnant woman, and they will not escape. But you are not in darkness, brothers, for that day to surprise you like a thief. For you are all children of light, children of the day. We are not of the night or of the darkness. So then let us not sleep, as others do, but let us keep awake and be sober. For those who sleep, sleep at night, and those who get drunk, are drunk at night. But since we belong to the day, let us be sober, having put on the breastplate of faith and love, and for a helmet the hope of salvation. ~ 1 Thessalonians 5:2-8

We often think of Advent as preparing for Christmas, and that is correct. However, even more, Advent is preparing for the Second Coming of Christ in glory at the end of time. *That* is what we need to be ready for. *That* determines where we will spend eternity. Scripture tells us that we must be prepared at all times, because we will not know when Jesus is coming. Let us keep awake and be sober, Paul tells us. It may seem like we have plenty of time to get right with God, but He could come tonight, and we must not be found sleeping.

Lord God, empower me by the Holy Spirit to be awake and sober always in readiness for the Coming of Jesus in glory at the end of time. In the name of my blessed Lord and Savior Jesus I pray. Amen.

Monday in the First Week in Advent

As it is written in Isaiah the prophet,
"Behold, I send my messenger before your face,
who will prepare your way,
the voice of one crying in the wilderness:
'Prepare the way of the Lord,
make his paths straight,'"

John appeared, baptizing in the wilderness and proclaiming a baptism of repentance for the forgiveness of sins. And all the country of Judea and all Jerusalem were going out to him and were being baptized by him in the river Jordan, confessing their sins. Now John was clothed with camel's hair and wore a leather belt around his waist and ate locusts and wild honey. And he preached, saying, "After me comes he who is mightier than I, the strap of whose sandals I am not worthy to stoop down and untie. I have baptized you with water, but he will baptize you with the Holy Spirit." ~ Mark 1:2-8

John the Baptist prepared the way for Jesus's earthly ministry, calling people to repentance. Each of us is called not only to repent of our own sins but also to prepare the way for the Second Coming of the Lord. We are called to share the Gospel with the whole world so no one will miss out on salvation. When Jesus comes, it will be too late. We have to decide for ourselves and share with others, so they have a chance to decide whether or not to follow Him.

Lord God, I have decided to follow You, and I intend to be ready when Jesus comes again. But I haven't done a very good job of giving others the opportunity to decide to follow Him. Forgive me for not sharing the Gospel with everyone I come in contact with. Don't let someone else miss out on the chance for eternity with You because they never heard the Gospel. Show me opportunities to witness personally and the opportunities to support missionaries who share the Gospel with people I will never meet. In the name of Jesus Christ. Amen.

Tuesday in the First Week in Advent

And the crowds asked him [John the Baptist], "What then shall we do?" And he answered them, "Whoever has two tunics is to share with him who has none, and whoever has food is to do likewise." Tax collectors also came to be baptized and said to him, "Teacher, what shall we do?" And he said to them, "Collect no more than you are authorized to do." Soldiers also asked him, "And we, what shall we do?" And he said to them, "Do not extort money from anyone by threats or by false accusation, and be content with your wages." ~ Luke 3:10-14

John the Baptist had specific things for each person to do, depending on their situations. Those who had worldly goods were told to share. Those who profited from collecting more for taxes than were due and pocketing the rest were told to do their job and collect the right amount of tax. Soldiers were told to do their jobs and not take advantage of their power to extort money. What would John the Baptist tell each of us today? Whatever specifics he would give, the bottom line would be to love our neighbors. The first great commandment is to love God with all our hearts, minds, and strength, and the second is to love our neighbors as ourselves. If we truly did that, we would not do any of the things that John was telling people to turn from.

Lord God, You know my heart and my sins. Turn me from putting myself before others. Teach me to love my neighbor as myself. Motivate and empower me by the Spirit to give rather than take, comfort rather than irritate, and do right rather than wrong. In the name of Jesus Christ, my Lord and Savior. Amen.

Wednesday in the First Week in Advent

And the haughtiness of man shall be humbled, and the lofty pride of men shall be brought low, and the Lord alone will be exalted in that day. ~ Isaiah 2:17

How haughty and prideful we are. We tend to think that our accomplishments are due to our own cleverness, forgetting that anything we have is a gift from God. Some of us are proud of our appearance, others of our intelligence, and others of artistic skill or computer wizardry. We're even proud of our humility! When we face the Lord, though, we will all be humbled and brought low. Only God is worthy of worship. Only the Lord deserves our praise, honor, and glory. Only our Triune God will be exalted when every knee will bow and every tongue confess that Jesus Christ is Lord.

Forgive me, Lord, for my pride. Forgive me for failing to give You all the glory. Humble me and bring me low as I deserve so that I exalt and worship You as You deserve. In the holy name of Jesus. Amen.

Thursday in the First Week in Advent

Lift up your heads, O gates!
And be lifted up, O ancient doors,
that the King of glory may come in.
Who is this King of glory?
The Lord, strong and mighty,
the Lord, mighty in battle!
Lift up your heads, O gates!
And lift them up, O ancient doors,
that the King of glory may come in.
Who is this King of glory?
The Lord of hosts,
he is the King of glory!
~ Psalm 24:7-10

This is one of my favorite Scripture passages, even though it seems a little strange to be telling gates and doors to lift their heads. The imagery is powerful to show the might, power, and glory of the Lord of lords and King of kings. I can visualize huge ancient gates to a city opening wide or maybe high if they are lifted up, opening their full width and height for the Lord of hosts, the King of glory. That's how God wants us to open our hearts—wide and high and full of welcome. May it be so!

Lord of lords and King of kings, let me open my heart as high and wide as the most magnificent ancient gates ever opened for an earthly king. Let my open heart welcome the King of glory, to be compelled to worship You on Christmas and every day. Give me a grateful heart for Your many blessings to me, my family, and friends. In the name of Jesus Christ, our Lord. Amen.

Friday in the First Week in Advent

Woe to those who call evil good
and good evil,
who put darkness for light
and light for darkness,
who put bitter for sweet
and sweet for bitter!
Woe to those who are wise in their own eyes,
and shrewd in their own sight!
Woe to those who are heroes at drinking wine,
and valiant men in mixing strong drink,
who acquit the guilty for a bribe,
and deprive the innocent of his right!
~ Isaiah 5:20-23

This sounds like a description of our society today —
good being called evil and evil being called good. So
many people are wise in their own eyes, but their *wisdom*
is contrary to Scripture. True wisdom comes from God
and is contained in His Word. Anything contrary to that
is man trying to put himself in God's place. May we
always recognize our own foolishness and God's
wisdom.

*God, Who is filled with wisdom, help me to always make my
decisions on Your Word and not my own knowledge. Guide
those in positions of authority to lean on Your wisdom and
guidance to protect innocent lives in the womb and others who
are weak and vulnerable. Open the hearts and minds of people
to know good and evil — to do good and to abstain from evil.
Bring a revival to this country, O Lord. In the name of Jesus
Christ. Amen.*

Saturday in the First Week in Advent

Therefore the Lord himself will give you a sign. Behold, the virgin shall conceive and bear a son, and shall call his name Immanuel. He shall eat curds and honey when he knows how to refuse the evil and choose the good. ~ Isaiah 7:14-15

Centuries before the birth of Jesus, God's prophet was telling His people what would come. Immanuel means "God with us," and Jesus came to earth to be with each of us who love and follow Him. God has told us what will come in the future. Jesus will come again in glory, majesty, and power. He is with us now in our hearts, but in that great day, we will be with Him in Heaven forever and ever and ever.

Lord God, we are ready for the return of Jesus. Maranatha, Lord Jesus!

The Second Sunday in Advent

In the sixth month the angel Gabriel was sent from God to a city of Galilee named Nazareth, to a virgin betrothed to a man whose name was Joseph, of the house of David. And the virgin's name was Mary. And he came to her and said, "Greetings, O favored one, the Lord is with you!" But she was greatly troubled at the saying, and tried to discern what sort of greeting this might be. And the angel said to her, "Do not be afraid, Mary, for you have found favor with God. And behold, you will conceive in your womb and bear a son, and you shall call his name Jesus. He will be great and will be called the Son of the Most High.

7

And the Lord God will give to him the throne of his father David, and he will reign over the house of Jacob forever, and of his kingdom there will be no end."

And Mary said to the angel, "How will this be, since I am a virgin?"

And the angel answered her, "The Holy Spirit will come upon you, and the power of the Most High will overshadow you; therefore the child to be born will be called holy—the Son of God. And behold, your relative Elizabeth in her old age has also conceived a son, and this is the sixth month with her who was called barren. For nothing will be impossible with God." And Mary said, "Behold, I am the servant of the Lord; let it be to me according to your word." And the angel departed from her. ~ Luke 1:26-38

I always want to be like Mary—saying, "I am the servant of the Lord; let it be to me according to your word." But I'm not always so responsive when I feel God calling me to do something. First, I doubt the call—God didn't put that idea in my head. Then when it's confirmed, such as a specific verse or word bombarding me everywhere, I make up excuses. I eventually give in, but why do I resist? Perhaps it's because I don't think I'm qualified, and in truth I'm not qualified. But if God calls me to a task, He will equip me to do it. Maybe I fear it's going to be difficult, but that's a good reason to get started right away to have plenty of time to do it. Would I react differently if an angel appeared with a message from God? I need to remember Mary's response when she was called to something much bigger than I'll ever be called on to do. Whatever He calls me to do, my answer should always be, "I am the Lord's servant; let Your will be done."

Lord God, forgive me for the times I have hesitated and resisted when You have given me something to do for You. Whether it's joining the intercessory prayer team, writing a book of devotionals, or simply showing up when I don't feel like it, let me always respond with an immediate yes and whatever action You ask of me. In the name of Jesus Christ, my Lord and Savior. Amen.

Monday in the Second Week in Advent

Bind up the testimony; seal the teaching among my disciples. I will wait for the Lord, who is hiding his face from the house of Jacob, and I will hope in him. ~ Isaiah 8:16-17

God was "hiding his face from the house of Jacob" because of the sinfulness of the people and the leadership. But God's promises didn't go away. The prophet would wait for the Lord because he still had hope in the Lord. So often when things don't go our way, we think God has turned His face from us. Sometimes Christians begin to have doubts and even think they should turn their own face away from God. But Isaiah knows, and we know in our deepest hearts, that God has not abandoned us. His promises are still true. We are still His children. He still loves us, and He still has a plan for our future and our welfare.

Almighty God, forgive me when I doubt Your promises or when I begin to lose hope. I know Your promises are forever true, and my hope in You is never misplaced. Let me give You no reason to turn Your face from me, but when things don't go

9

my way, help me to remember that Your ways are higher than my ways, Your thoughts higher than my thoughts. Many times in my life I have discovered that what seemed bad when it happened worked out to be good. Thank You that You work all things for good to those who love You and are called according to Your purpose. In the name of my Lord and Savior, Jesus Christ. Amen.

Tuesday in the Second Week in Advent

What will you do on the day of punishment,
in the ruin that will come from afar?
To whom will you flee for help,
and where will you leave your wealth?
Nothing remains but to crouch among the prisoners
or fall among the slain.
For all this his anger has not turned away,
and his hand is stretched out still.
~ Isaiah 10:3-4

Those who have not accepted Jesus as their Lord and Savior will face God's wrath. Wealth, fame, physical strength, intellect, earthly power—none of these will save. Only the blood of Jesus can save, and that requires belief and confession. Every knee will bow and every tongue confess that Jesus is Lord, but if not done freely before He comes again in glory, it will be too late.

Lord God, I confess that Jesus is my Lord and Savior. His blood covers my sin. Otherwise I would be condemned to the everlasting lake of fire. Thank You that You love us enough to send Jesus to take our sins and give us a way to obtain righteousness – not by our own actions but by His sacrifice.

Empower me by the Holy Spirit to live my life in a way that brings You honor. In the name of Jesus. Amen.

Wednesday in the Second Week in Advent

There shall come forth a shoot from the stump of Jesse, and a branch from his roots shall bear fruit. And the Spirit of the Lord shall rest upon him, the Spirit of wisdom and understanding, the Spirit of counsel and might, the Spirit of knowledge and the fear of the Lord. And his delight shall be in the fear of the Lord. He shall not judge by what his eyes see, or decide disputes by what his ears hear, but with righteousness he shall judge the poor, and decide with equity for the meek of the earth; and he shall strike the earth with the rod of his mouth, and with the breath of his lips he shall kill the wicked. Righteousness shall be the belt of his waist, and faithfulness the belt of his loins. The wolf shall dwell with the lamb, and the leopard shall lie down with the young goat, and the calf and the lion and the fattened calf together; and a little child shall lead them. The cow and the bear shall graze; their young shall lie down together; and the lion shall eat straw like the ox. The nursing child shall play over the hole of the cobra, and the weaned child shall put his hand on the adder's den. They shall not hurt or destroy in all my holy mountain; for the earth shall be full of the knowledge of the Lord as the waters cover the sea. In that day the root of Jesse, who shall stand as a signal for the peoples—of him shall the nations inquire, and his resting place shall be glorious.
~ Isaiah 11:1-10

When Jesus comes again in glory to rule His kingdom, everything described in this passage will come to pass. All God's creation will be at peace, the way He created it to be. There will no harm to anyone or anything because all will be filled with the knowledge of God. All, that is, who are in God's holy mountain, the new Jerusalem. He will judge righteously, but He will destroy the wicked with "the rod of his mouth and with the breath of his lips." I want to be with those who can put their hand in a snake's den and not be harmed. That will come from recognizing Jesus as Lord *before* He returns. Once He arrives in glory, it will be too late.

Thank You, Lord, that You are giving everyone a chance to come to You, to confess Jesus as Lord, to receive forgiveness of sins and eternal salvation. Help me to spread Your Word so that many who don't know You will come to know You before it's too late. Open my mouth to say the words You want me to say to people I come in contact with, and open my heart to support those who take the Gospel to unreached people, whether they are in faraway lands or in our own neighborhoods. In the name of Jesus Christ. Amen.

Thursday in the Second Week in Advent

Behold, the day of the Lord comes, cruel, with wrath and fierce anger, to make the land a desolation and to destroy its sinners from it. For the stars of the heavens and their constellations will not give their light; the sun will be dark at its rising, and the moon will not shed its light. I will punish the world for its evil, and the wicked for their iniquity; I will put an end to the pomp of the arrogant, and lay low the pompous pride of the ruthless. ~ Isaiah 13:9-11

This passage reminds us that while God is love — He loves us so much that Jesus died so every single person on earth can have eternal life if they choose to follow Jesus—God is also just. He will punish the wicked and destroy sinners. On the Judgement Day, I want to be among those to whom Jesus says, "Well done, good and faithful servant. Enter into the joy of your Master." I do *not* want to be among those who are tossed into the lake of fire. The choice is ours.

Lord God, thank You for Your plan of salvation. You are giving us all a chance at eternal life, delaying Jesus's return to give sinners time to repent and turn to You. But the day will come when the chance is gone. Help me to share the Gospel with others and support ministries and missionaries so that as many as possible come to faith before it is too late. In the precious name of Jesus. Amen.

Friday in the Second Week in Advent

On that day the Lord will punish the host of heaven, in heaven, and the kings of the earth, on the earth. They will be gathered together as prisoners in a pit; they will be shut up in a prison, and after many days they will be punished.
~ Isaiah 24:21-22

This passage confused me, so I read several commentaries on it. There are several theories about the "host of heaven, in heaven" (ESV and NRSV) or "host of the high ones that are on high" (KJV) or "host of heaven on high" (NASB) or "the powers in the heavens above" (NIV). They may be the sun, moon, and stars or their idols that were worshipped. They may be the spiritual forces of evil in heavenly places that Paul talks about. Or they may be the ecclesiastical leaders of the Jews. But whichever commentator is correct, we know they are powerful and evil. The kings of the earth, on the earth, are obviously powerful earthly rulers. Whoever and whatever thinks they are powerful will find out just how little power they really have. They will be gathered together and punished.

Lord God, we know You are a God of love. Often we focus on Your forgiveness, forgetting that we must repent and turn to Jesus to receive forgiveness. We need to be reminded that You are also a God of justice, and You will punish the wicked, no matter how powerful and "important" they are in earthly terms. In the name of Jesus Christ, our Lord and Savior, who reigns with You and the Holy Ghost, world without end. Amen.

Saturday in the Second Week in Advent

Therefore thus says the Lord God, "Behold, I am the one who has laid as a foundation in Zion, a stone, a tested stone, a precious cornerstone, of a sure foundation: 'Whoever believes will not be in haste.' And I will make justice the line, and righteousness the plumb line; and hail will sweep away the refuge of lies, and waters will overwhelm the shelter." ~ Isaiah 28:16-17

God laid the "precious cornerstone" of Jesus Christ, and His Kingdom is a kingdom of justice and righteousness. A plumb line shows that a building is straight and true. In God's Kingdom, justice is a straight line and righteousness is a plumb line, ensuring there is no wavering. We can be sure our foundation is strong when we build our lives with Jesus as the cornerstone.

Father God, I don't want my life to waver from Your straight line of justice and righteousness. Jesus is the Lord of my life, and I can trust that my foundation is strong. Thank You for giving us such a strong foundation. In His name we pray. Amen.

The Third Sunday in Advent

Then the eyes of the blind shall be opened, and the ears of the deaf unstopped; then shall the lame man leap like a deer, and the tongue of the mute sing for joy. For waters break forth in the wilderness, and streams in the desert; the burning sand shall become a pool, and the thirsty ground springs of water; in the haunt of jackals, where they lie down, the grass shall become reeds and rushes. And a highway shall be there, and it shall be called the Way of Holiness; the unclean shall not pass over it. It shall belong to those who walk on the way; even if they are fools, they shall not go astray. ~ Isaiah 35:5-8

The beginning of the passage describes a place we'd like to be—no more disabilities or illnesses, lots of water and greenery, and the Way of Holiness, where nothing unclean can pass. Since by God's standards all of us are unclean, who can walk on that highway? Those who have been washed clean by the Blood of Christ, those who have Christ's righteousness imputed to them because of their faith in Him. And I love the last

15

sentence: even if we are fools, we will not go astray. We don't have to be smart in the ways of the world. We don't have to pay a fortune. We don't have to *do* anything but trust in Jesus. When we belong to Him, He doesn't let us stray off the path.

Thank You, Lord God, that You see me as righteous because the Blood of Jesus washed me clean. My sin would condemn me if You judged by my thoughts, words, deeds, and attitudes. I fall so short of Your standard, and I am so sorry. Yet You have forgiven all my sins — past, present, and future. Thank You that You won't let me go astray. In the precious name of Jesus. Amen.

Monday in the Third Week in Advent

Ah, you who hide deep from the Lord your counsel, whose deeds are in the dark, and who say, "Who sees us? Who knows us?" You turn things upside down! Shall the potter be regarded as the clay, that the thing made should say of its maker, "He did not make me"; or the thing formed say of him who formed it, "He has no understanding"? ~ Isaiah 29:15-16

I cringe when I hear someone say, "My God wouldn't send anyone to Hell" or "Jesus hung out with sinners — He's not judgmental." That's the clay saying it doesn't need the potter, as if a pot can form itself or know more than the potter. God is described in the Bible, and no matter how we try to change the meaning of His Word, He will judge us, and not everyone will go to Heaven. Everyone has the choice, but if we rebel against Him in our earthly lives, we won't be with Him in Heaven. Yes,

Jesus loved and lived among sinners, but He didn't condone their sin. He said, "Go and sin no more."

Lord God, wash away our pride and arrogance. You made us, and You understand us completely, yet we often act as if we think we know better than You. Remind us that You are the potter, and we are the clay. You formed us, and You have a plan for us. Show us the way You want us to go. In the name of Jesus Christ, our Lord and Savior. Amen.

Tuesday after the Third Sunday in Advent

Then I heard what seemed to be the voice of a great multitude, like the roar of many waters and like the sound of mighty peals of thunder, crying out, "Hallelujah! For the Lord our God the Almighty reigns. Let us rejoice and exult and give him the glory, for the marriage of the Lamb has come, and his Bride has made herself ready; it was granted her to clothe herself with fine linen, bright and pure"— for the fine linen is the righteous deeds of the saints. ~ Revelation 19:6-8

The day will come—we know not when—that Jesus marries His bride, the Church. If Jesus is our Lord, we are part of the Church who is Jesus's bride. We look at ourselves, at our sins, and we wonder how we could ever be clothed in righteous deeds or how we could be called a saint. Yet Scripture says that the bride will be dressed in bright and pure fine linen, the righteous deeds of the saints. That righteousness does not come from ourselves. The righteousness that is the bright and pure fine linen in which we will be clothed is the righteousness of Jesus. The Bridegroom gives everything

17

to the bride. All the bride has to do is to love Jesus and worship Him as Lord, follow where He leads.

Heavenly Father, we are making ourselves ready for the marriage of the Lamb by trusting in Him. Clothe us in the fine linen of the righteousness of Christ and lead us in Your way everlasting. In the name of Jesus Christ, who was, and is, and is to come. Amen.

Wednesday after the Third Sunday in Advent

"Stay dressed for action and keep your lamps burning, and be like men who are waiting for their master to come home from the wedding feast, so that they may open the door to him at once when he comes and knocks. Blessed are those servants whom the master finds awake when he comes. Truly, I say to you, he will dress himself for service and have them recline at table, and he will come and serve them. If he comes in the second watch, or in the third, and finds them awake, blessed are those servants! But know this, that if the master of the house had known at what hour the thief was coming, he would not have left his house to be broken into. You also must be ready, for the Son of Man is coming at an hour you do not expect." ~ Luke 12:35-40

A friend and I were discussing the Second Coming. She said, and I tend to agree, that we are approaching that day. We see many things happening now that are among the signs that Jesus told us we would see. However, He also told us that no one knows, that He will come like a thief in the night. He may not return for thousands of years—or He may return tonight. We cannot become complacent and think that we have lots of time. We must

18

be prepared for His coming again in glory. There's only one thing we can do to be ready: accept Jesus as our Lord and Savior. We can never be righteous enough to earn our way into Heaven. On the other hand, if we lead a sinful, unrepentant life, we aren't going to get there either. We are sinful by nature, and we will continue to sin. But we repent of our sins and ask His forgiveness and not willingly continue to sin. If we continue to sin willfully and deliberately, we haven't truly accepted Jesus as Lord. We haven't truly submitted our will to His.

O Lord, our God, empower us by the Holy Spirit to be ready when Jesus comes again. Whether he comes early or late, let Him find us awake, dressed, with our lamps burning, waiting for His return. In His name. Amen.

Thursday after the Third Sunday in Advent

Let the heavens be glad, and let the earth rejoice;
let the sea roar, and all that fills it;
let the field exult, and everything in it!
Then shall all the trees of the forest sing for joy
before the Lord, for he comes,
for he comes to judge the earth.
He will judge the world in righteousness,
and the peoples in his faithfulness.
~ Psalm 96:11-13

Elsewhere in Scripture (Joel 2:11), we read "For the day of the Lord is great and very awesome; who can endure it?" In Revelation, we read about the Great Tribulation. Even Jesus talked about terrible tribulation before His coming. But the psalmist tells us and all of nature to be glad and rejoice, to exult and sing for joy, when the Lord comes to judge the world and its people. Why? Because He judges in righteousness and faithfulness, and if we are His, there will be an end to the curse, an end to pain and sorrow, an end to sin and evil. The ones who won't rejoice are those who rejected Him in this life. He will judge them and send them to eternal punishment for their sin that was not washed away by the Blood of Jesus.

Lord, too often we think of judgment as something bad. We fear the Judgment Day when You will judge the world. But we know You judge with righteousness and faithfulness, and we know that You forgive the sins of those who accept Jesus as their Savior and who truly and earnestly repent of their sins. With Jesus as our Advocate, we need not fear Your judgment, for He has washed us whiter than snow. We will be glad and rejoice that He is coming to judge the world and the people with truth. In His name. Amen.

Friday after the Third Sunday in Advent

I have fought the good fight, I have finished the race, I have kept the faith. Henceforth there is laid up for me the crown of righteousness, which the Lord, the righteous judge, will award to me on that Day, and not only to me but also to all who have loved his appearing. ~ 2 Timothy 4:7-8

Paul could say with confidence that he had fought the good fight, finished the race, and kept the faith. Can the same be said of us? Sometimes it seems too hard to stand strong in the face of a culture that devalues faith and even life. We may be ridiculed and insulted for not being *politically correct*. We may suffer consequences, such as having our business sued for *intolerance* for doing what is right. We may lose friends or anger family members who choose to live a sinful lifestyle and expect us not only to tolerate it but to approve of it. But if we want the crown of righteousness, we must stay strong. We must stay in the fight in spite of ridicule and insults, despite legal or financial or relationship consequences.

Heavenly Father, guide us by the Holy Spirit to fight the good fight, finish the race, keep the faith so that, along with Paul and the other saints, we will be awarded the crown of righteousness. In the name of Jesus Christ, our Lord and Savior. Amen.

Saturday after the Third Sunday in Advent

"Behold, I send my messenger, and he will prepare the way before me. And the Lord whom you seek will suddenly come to his temple; and the messenger of the covenant in whom you delight, behold, he is coming, says the Lord of hosts. But who can endure the day of his coming, and who can stand when he appears? For he is like a refiner's fire and like fullers' soap. He will sit as a refiner and purifier of silver, and he will purify the sons of Levi and refine them like gold and silver, and they will bring offerings in righteousness to the Lord. ~ Malachi 3:1-3

Jesus is coming, and He will refine and purify us, as a silversmith refines and purifies silver. The silversmith knows that the silver is refined and pure when he can

21

see his own face reflected in the silver. May we be purified and refined until Jesus can see Himself in us.

O holy Lord, refine us in Your fire, cleanse us with Your soap – the Blood of the Lamb. Make us as pure as the purest gold and silver refined in the hottest fire. Make us ready to stand in the day of Jesus' return. In His name. Amen.

The Fourth Sunday in Advent

Comfort, comfort my people, says your God. Speak tenderly to Jerusalem, and cry to her that her warfare is ended, that her iniquity is pardoned, that she has received from the Lord's hand double for all her sins. A voice cries: "In the wilderness prepare the way of the Lord; make straight in the desert a highway for our God. Every valley shall be lifted up, and every mountain and hill be made low; the uneven ground shall become level, and the rough places a plain. And the glory of the Lord shall be revealed, and all flesh shall see it together, for the mouth of the Lord has spoken." A voice says, "Cry!" And I said, "What shall I cry?" All flesh is grass, and all its beauty is like the flower of the field. The grass withers, the flower fades when the breath of the Lord blows on it; surely the people are grass. The grass withers, the flower fades, but the word of our God will stand forever. Get you up to a high mountain, O Zion, herald of good news; lift up your voice with strength, O Jerusalem, herald of good news; lift it up, fear not; say to the cities of Judah, "Behold your God!" Behold, the Lord God comes with might, and his arm rules for him; behold, his reward is with him, and his recompense before him. He will tend his flock like a shepherd; he will gather the lambs in his arms; he will carry them in his bosom, and gently lead those that are with young. ~ Isaiah 40:1-11

Long before Jesus was born, Isaiah told the Jewish people the Lord was coming in might. A tiny baby born in a stable isn't our idea of might, but that's how our Lord came as one of us. The Creator who made us, the Almighty Ruler of the Universe who is sovereign over us, chose to become one of us in order to become our Savior, the one who tends his flock like a shepherd. When He comes again, He will come in might and judgment. Let us prepare His way. Let us share the good news. Let us behold our God!

Lord, prepare our hearts for You; make straight a pathway for us to receive You. Reveal Yourself to us that we may behold You in all Your glory and worship You in adoration. In the name of Jesus Christ, our Lord and Savior, who lives and reigns with the Father and the Holy Ghost, now and forever. Amen.

Monday after the Fourth Sunday in Advent

And Mary said,
"My soul magnifies the Lord,
and my spirit rejoices in God my Savior,
for he has looked on the humble estate of his servant.
For behold, from now on all generations will call me blessed;
for he who is mighty has done great things for me,
and holy is his name.
And his mercy is for those who fear him
from generation to generation.

23

He has shown strength with his arm;
he has scattered the proud in the thoughts of their hearts;
he has brought down the mighty from their thrones
and exalted those of humble estate;
he has filled the hungry with good things,
and the rich he has sent away empty.
He has helped his servant Israel,
in remembrance of his mercy,
as he spoke to our fathers,
to Abraham and to his offspring forever."
~ Luke 1:46-55

Every time I read these words, my mind automatically says the King James Version, no matter what I'm reading (as this ESV). The Magnificat is a canticle in the Evening Prayer service in the *1928 Book of Common Prayer*. Although I confess I don't read Evening Prayer every single night as intended, I love it—especially when we chant it at our midweek service at church. I wish I were as joyful, faithful, and poetic as Mary when faced with new and challenging circumstances, but unfortunately, my first thoughts aren't always so noble. Oh, that I would be more like her!

Heavenly Father, Mary was so young and faced with a situation that must have been confusing and frightening. Yet she praised You and recognized that Your plan was perfect. Give us that kind of faith – to praise You in all circumstances, even those that are frightening and confusing. In the name of Jesus Christ, our Lord and Savior, who lives and reigns with You and the Holy Ghost, ever one God, world without end. Amen.

Tuesday after the Fourth Sunday in Advent

No longer will there be anything accursed, but the throne of God and of the Lamb will be in it, and his servants will worship him. They will see his face, and his name will be on their foreheads. And night will be no more. They will need no light of lamp or sun, for the Lord God will be their light, and they will reign forever and ever. And he said to me, "These words are trustworthy and true. And the Lord, the God of the spirits of the prophets, has sent his angel to show his servants what must soon take place." "And behold, I am coming soon. Blessed is the one who keeps the words of the prophecy of this book." ~ Revelation 22:3-7

Revelation can be very confusing and hard to understand. But this passage is clear: Those of us who love the Lord and have accepted Jesus as our Savior will spend eternity in Heaven, where Jesus will be. We will see His face in the light of eternal day, for God is the light that outshines the sun and all the stars. God the Father and Jesus our Lord will reign forever and ever and ever. Jesus is coming soon!

Praise God that Jesus is coming. Maranatha, Lord Jesus! Amen.

Wednesday after the Fourth Sunday in Advent

For the grace of God has appeared, bringing salvation for all people, training us to renounce ungodliness and worldly passions, and to live self-controlled, upright, and godly lives in the present age, waiting for our blessed hope, the appearing of the glory of our great God and Savior Jesus Christ, who gave himself for us to redeem us from all lawlessness and to purify for himself a people for his own possession who are zealous for good works. ~ Titus 2:11-14

The grace of God trains us for upright and godly lives while we wait for the return of Jesus. We can live godly lives because Jesus Himself redeemed us from all wickedness and cleaned and purified us with His blood. We are His people and because we love Him and worship Him and adore Him for His great sacrifice, we want to do what is good. He forgives our sins, but our desire is to do good and not evil for His sake.

Lord, we wait for the blessed hope of Jesus' return. Teach us to say "No" to worldly passions and to live self-controlled and righteous lives. In Jesus' name. Amen.

Christmas Eve

Now the birth of Jesus Christ took place in this way. When his mother Mary had been betrothed to Joseph, before they came together she was found to be with child from the Holy Spirit. And her husband Joseph, being a just man and unwilling to put her to shame, resolved to divorce her quietly. But as he considered these things, behold, an angel of the Lord appeared to him in a dream, saying, "Joseph, son of David, do not fear to take Mary as your wife, for that which is conceived in her is from the Holy Spirit. She will bear a son, and you shall call his name Jesus, for he will save his people from their sins." All this took place to fulfill what the Lord had spoken by the prophet:

"Behold, the virgin shall conceive and bear a son,
and they shall call his name Immanuel"

(which means, God with us). When Joseph woke from sleep, he did as the angel of the Lord commanded him: he took his wife, but knew her not until she had given birth to a son. And he called his name Jesus. ~ Matthew 1:18-25

We honor Mary for being the mother of our Lord, but sometimes we fail to recognize Joseph's part. First, he thought his espoused had been unfaithful. When she told him she was pregnant, he knew he wasn't the father, so he naturally assumed that she had been unfaithful. The Lord sent an angel to Joseph in a dream to tell him the truth, and from then on, Joseph cared for Mary and raised Jesus as his own. People would have assumed that he and Mary had anticipated their wedding, yet he accepted whatever scandal there was and followed everything God told him to do.

Heavenly Father, we praise You and bless You for sending Your Son Jesus Christ to save us from our sins. Immanuel – God with us! Father, Son, and Holy Spirit with us always and forever – thank You! And thank You that Mary and Joseph were faithful in carrying out Your will to make Immanuel possible. In the name of Jesus Christ, Your Son, our Lord and Savior, who lives and reigns with You and the Holy Spirit, ever one God, world without end. Amen.

Christmas Day

The Word became flesh and made his dwelling among us.

John 1:14

In the beginning was the Word, and the Word was with God, and the Word was God. He was in the beginning with God. All things were made through him, and without him was not any thing made that was made. In him was life, and the life was the light of men. The light shines in the darkness, and the darkness has not overcome it.

There was a man sent from God, whose name was John. He came as a witness, to bear witness about the light, that all might believe through him. He was not the light, but came to bear witness about the light.

The true light, which enlightens everyone, was coming into the world. He was in the world, and the world was made through him, yet the world did not know him. He came to his own, and his own people did not receive him. But to all who did receive him, who believed in his name, he gave the right to become children of God, who were born, not of blood nor of the will of the flesh nor of the will of man, but of God.

And the Word became flesh and dwelt among us, and we have seen his glory, glory as of the only Son from the Father, full of grace and truth. ~ John 1:1-14

This is one of my favorite Scriptures. John doesn't describe Jesus's birth as a tiny baby. He doesn't talk about shepherds and angels and a stable. He reminds us Who it was that came into the world—the Word, God, the Creator, always existing, the Light of the World. *That* is Who humbled Himself to leave His throne in Heaven and come to earth as one of us. There's sometimes a question as to which is most important— Christmas or Easter. But I heard in a homily the truth that without the incarnation at Christmas, there would be no resurrection, no Easter. God's entire plan of salvation hinged on that tiny baby born on Christmas Day.

Lord God Almighty, thank You for the incarnation of Your Son, our Lord. He was born to die for our sins and because of His sacrifice, we live. We are amazed at how much You love us. Give us grateful hearts and empower us to live for Your glory. In the name of Jesus Christ, who lives and reigns with you and the Holy Ghost, now and forever. Amen.

The Second Day of Christmas

And in the same region there were shepherds out in the field, keeping watch over their flock by night. And an angel of the Lord appeared to them, and the glory of the Lord shone around them, and they were filled with great fear. And the angel said to them, "Fear not, for behold, I bring you good news of great joy that will be for all the people. For unto you is born this day in the city of David a Savior, who is Christ the Lord. And this will be a sign for you: you will find a baby wrapped in swaddling cloths and lying in a manger." And suddenly there was with the angel a multitude of the heavenly host praising God and saying,

"Glory to God in the highest,
    and on earth peace among those with whom he is pleased!"

When the angels went away from them into heaven, the shepherds said to one another, "Let us go over to Bethlehem and see this thing that has happened, which the Lord has made known to us." And they went with haste and found Mary and Joseph, and the baby lying in a manger. And when they saw it, they made known the saying that had been told them concerning this child. And all who heard it wondered at what the shepherds told them. But Mary treasured up all these things, pondering them in her heart. And the shepherds returned, glorifying and praising God for all they had heard and seen, as it had been told them. ~ Luke 2:8-20

Most people would expect angels to announce the birth of the Savior of the World to royalty or aristocrats or "important" people. Instead the first people to hear of the birth of the Messiah from the angelic choir were shepherds, not exactly high society. They slept outside under the stars with dirty, smelly animals and didn't have daily showers and laundry service. But in the Kingdom of God, they merited the visit from the angels. It should make us all realize that no matter how wealthy or poor, how esteemed or maligned, how old or how young, we are equally important to the Lord.

Thank You, Lord, that You esteem lowly shepherds as much — or more — than kings or military leaders or people with the respect of society. Thank You that You love each of us as much as You love anyone else. Each of us is precious in Your sight, and Jesus came to bear the sins of us all, if only we will repent and follow Him. In His name we pray. Amen.

The Third Day of Christmas

This is the message we have heard from him and proclaim to you, that God is light, and in him is no darkness at all. If we say we have fellowship with him while we walk in darkness, we lie and do not practice the truth. But if we walk in the light, as he is in the light, we have fellowship with one another, and the blood of Jesus his Son cleanses us from all sin. If we say we have no sin, we deceive ourselves, and the truth is not in us. If we confess our sins, he is faithful and just to forgive us our sins and to cleanse us from all unrighteousness. ~ 1 John 1:5-9

We are sinful, but we can still walk in the Light of God. If we deny our sin, we remain in darkness, but if we confess and repent, He will not only forgive our sins, but He will also cleanse us. He will take away our unrighteousness and cover us with the righteousness of Christ, and we will walk in Christ. How amazing is that! God sees us as pure and holy as Jesus if we are covered by His blood.

Lord God, in my humanity I am filled with sin. As the confession for daily morning and evening prayer in the prayer book says, we are "miserable offenders" and "there is no health in us." Yet You wipe away our sins and pardon our offenses if we call on the name of Jesus. I do confess and repent, O Lord. Thank You for Your forgiveness and for seeing me as You see Jesus. In His name I pray. Amen.

The Fourth Day of Christmas (Holy Innocents)

Then Herod, when he saw that he had been tricked by the wise men, became furious, and he sent and killed all the male

children in Bethlehem and in all that region who were two years old or under, according to the time that he had ascertained from the wise men. Then was fulfilled what was spoken by the prophet Jeremiah:
"A voice was heard in Ramah,
  weeping and loud lamentation,
Rachel weeping for her children;
  she refused to be comforted, because they are no more." ~ Matthew 2:16-18

It's hard to envision the slaughter of the innocent young children that Herod ordered. He was so power-hungry that he wouldn't take a chance that a tiny child would grow up to become king in Herod's place. So he murdered the innocent and broke the hearts of their families. Yet today it is legal—and in the minds of many people perfectly acceptable for equally selfish reasons — to kill innocent babies before they leave the womb. Perhaps the mother is afraid because she doesn't have a support system. Maybe the child was conceived in rape or incest and the abuser forces the mother to abort. Or the mother might be a Christian who is embarrassed by an out-of-wedlock pregnancy and who is easily convinced to "get rid of the problem." I've read that 70% of abortions are performed on mothers who claim the name of Christ! None of these reasons are any better justification for killing babies than Herod's slaughter of the Holy Innocents.

Lord God, probably no one sees any justification for what Herod did, but far too many people see justification for the murder of innocents that is legal today. Forgive us for not stopping this abomination! Open the eyes of Your people and raise up leaders who will bring to an end to legalized abortion as Christians in earlier times brought an end to the institution of legal slavery. We beg this in the name of Jesus Christ, our Lord and Savior. Amen.

The Fifth Day of Christmas

And the Word became flesh and dwelt among us, and we have seen his glory, glory as of the only Son from the Father, full of grace and truth (John bore witness about him, and cried out, "This was he of whom I said, 'He who comes after me ranks before me, because he was before me.'") For from his fullness we have all received, grace upon grace. For the law was given through Moses; grace and truth came through Jesus Christ. No one has ever seen God; the only God, who is at the Father's side, he has made him known. ~ John 1:14-18

The Law was given in the past, but now Jesus has brought grace and truth. Unfortunately, some people take that grace as license to do whatever they want. Even though we're no longer governed by the Law, God still wants us to love Him with all our hearts, our souls, our strength, and our minds and to love our neighbors as ourselves. If we do those things, we will not steal, covet, murder, commit adultery, or any of the other prohibitions of the Law. We will avoid doing those things because of our love for our God and others—not because the Law says we shouldn't do them. Of course, as sinful human beings, we cannot do this on our own or perfectly, but the grace of God helps us to do them better than we could do on our own. And when we fall short, that same grace forgives us and wipes away our sins as if they never happened.

Thank You, Lord, for Your grace. I fall short so often, but without Your grace enabling me I would always be mired in sin. Thank You for Your grace in guiding me by the Holy Ghost in the times I do Your will and for Your grace in forgiving me when I miss the mark and repent. Help me to do Your will more and more. In the name of Jesus Christ, my Lord and Savior. Amen.

The Sixth Day of Christmas

After this I looked, and behold, a great multitude that no one could number, from every nation, from all tribes and peoples and languages, standing before the throne and before the Lamb, clothed in white robes, with palm branches in their hands, and crying out with a loud voice, "Salvation belongs to our God who sits on the throne, and to the Lamb!" And all the angels were standing around the throne and around the elders and the four living creatures, and they fell on their faces before the throne and worshiped God, saying, "Amen! Blessing and glory and wisdom and thanksgiving and honor and power and might be to our God forever and ever! Amen."

Then one of the elders addressed me, saying, "Who are these, clothed in white robes, and from where have they come?" I said to him, "Sir, you know." And he said to me, "These are the ones coming out of the great tribulation. They have washed their robes and made them white in the blood of the Lamb.

"Therefore they are before the throne of God,
  and serve him day and night in his temple;
  and he who sits on the throne will shelter them with his presence.
They shall hunger no more, neither thirst anymore;

the sun shall not strike them,
   nor any scorching heat.
For the Lamb in the midst of the throne will be their
shepherd,
   and he will guide them to springs of living water,
and God will wipe away every tear from their eyes."
~ Revelation 7:9-17

Imagine no more hunger or thirst, no more extreme
temperatures, no more tears! No more pain and
suffering, no more fear or sorrow, no more hurt or lack.
That is what we have to look forward to. When Jesus
comes again and takes all of His children with Him, we
will be as God created us to be. We will be free of the
shackles of sin.

*Father God, I look forward to the day when You will wipe
away every tear and ease all our pain. As St. Paul said, the
sufferings of the present time are not worthy of comparing to
the glory that awaits us. When I am in pain, help me to look
ahead to that future glory. In the name of Jesus Christ, my
Lord and Savior.*

The Seventh Day of Christmas

Now before faith came, we were held captive under the
law, imprisoned until the coming faith would be revealed. So
then, the law was our guardian until Christ came, in order that
we might be justified by faith. But now that faith has come,
we are no longer under a guardian, for in Christ Jesus you are
all sons of God, through faith. For as many of you as were
baptized into Christ have put on Christ. There is neither Jew
nor Greek, there is neither slave nor free, there is no male

and female, for you are all one in Christ Jesus. And if you are Christ's, then you are Abraham's offspring, heirs according to promise.

I mean that the heir, as long as he is a child, is no different from a slave, though he is the owner of everything, but he is under guardians and managers until the date set by his father. In the same way we also, when we were children, were enslaved to the elementary principles of the world. But when the fullness of time had come, God sent forth his Son, born of woman, born under the law, to redeem those who were under the law, so that we might receive adoption as sons. And because you are sons, God has sent the Spirit of his Son into our hearts, crying, "Abba! Father!" So you are no longer a slave, but a son, and if a son, then an heir through God. ~ Galatians 3:23-4:7

I don't understand God's plan or His timing. I'm just thankful that He has a perfect plan and perfect timing. We are no longer slaves but sons (and daughters!) of the King, brothers and sisters of Christ and of one another. None is more important or valuable than any other. God loves us all much more than we can even imagine.

Lord God, thank You that we who believe in Jesus and give our lives to Him are Your beloved children. Let me always recognize the value You place on my brothers and sisters and the love You have for each of them and let me love them as well. In the name of Jesus Christ. Amen.

The Eighth Day of Christmas (The Circumcision of Christ)

And at the end of eight days, when he was circumcised, he was called Jesus, the name given by the angel before he was conceived in the womb.

And when the time came for their purification according to the Law of Moses, they brought him up to Jerusalem to present him to the Lord (as it is written in the Law of the Lord, "Every male who first opens the womb shall be called holy to the Lord") and to offer a sacrifice according to what is said in the Law of the Lord, "a pair of turtledoves, or two young pigeons."

And when they had performed everything according to the Law of the Lord, they returned into Galilee, to their own town of Nazareth. And the child grew and became strong, filled with wisdom. And the favor of God was upon him.
~ Luke 2:21-24, 39-40

Even as a newborn baby, Jesus was the Messiah, the Christ, the Savior of the world, God Incarnate. And yet eight days after his birth, his parents took him to the temple to be circumcised and named. The angel had already told Mary His name before He was even conceived, but He went through the ritual as any other Jewish firstborn son. Sinners like us may resent rules, rituals, and regulations, but our Savior did not consider Himself above the law in spite of His divinity.

Lord, please forgive me when I'm impatient or resentful of Your laws and rituals. If Your Son, the Second Person of the Trinity, part of the Godhead, faithfully followed Your

commands, how much more important is it for me to do so!
Please help me through the Holy Spirit to be more like Jesus, in
Whose Name I pray. Amen.

The Ninth Day of Christmas

Now there was a man in Jerusalem, whose name was Simeon,
and this man was righteous and devout, waiting for the
consolation of Israel, and the Holy Spirit was upon him. And it
had been revealed to him by the Holy Spirit that he would not
see death before he had seen the Lord's Christ. And he came
in the Spirit into the temple, and when the parents brought in
the child Jesus, to do for him according to the custom of the
Law, he took him up in his arms and blessed God and said,

"Lord, now you are letting your servant depart in peace,
    according to your word;
for my eyes have seen your salvation
    that you have prepared in the presence of all peoples,
a light for revelation to the Gentiles,
    and for glory to your people Israel."

And his father and his mother marveled at what was said
about him. And Simeon blessed them and said to Mary his
mother, "Behold, this child is appointed for the fall and rising
of many in Israel, and for a sign that is opposed (and a sword
will pierce through your own soul also), so that thoughts from
many hearts may be revealed."

And there was a prophetess, Anna, the daughter of Phanuel,
of the tribe of Asher. She was advanced in years, having lived
with her husband seven years from when she was a virgin,
and then as a widow until she was eighty-four. She did not
depart from the temple, worshiping with fasting and prayer

night and day. And coming up at that very hour she began to give thanks to God and to speak of him to all who were waiting for the redemption of Jerusalem. ~ Luke 2:25-38

Simeon had been promised by God that he would see the Messiah, and he was led to come to the Temple when Joseph and Mary brought Jesus for His circumcision and naming. Anna was an elderly prophetess who had spent most of her adult life praying in the temple. Both of these faithful and long-time servants of God recognized the eight-day-old baby Jesus as the Messiah, the Christ, the Anointed One. They were so blessed to see the Savior in their lifetimes. We haven't held the tiny baby Jesus in our arms, but we can know Him as our Lord and Savior and as our truest and closest friend. We have the privilege of reading His Word and knowing the parables He told, the miracles He did, the sacrifice He made. Do we recognize our blessing as Simeon and Anna recognized Jesus?

Thank You, Father God, that we can know Jesus and through Him know You. You and Jesus, along with the Holy Spirit, created the world and everything in it. You are sovereign over the entire universe. You are powerful and mighty beyond our ability to imagine. Your ways are so far above our ways that we can't even recognize the good You are doing for us when life doesn't go the way we think it should. Yet You love each one of us more than human minds can comprehend. You want to know us personally, to hear our prayers and the deepest desires of our hearts. You want us to repent of our sins so You can shower us with forgiveness and spiritual blessings. Help us to know and to appreciate the magnitude of us ordinary people being loved and guided by the God of gods, the King of kings, the Lord of lords. We pray in the name of Jesus. Amen.

The Tenth Day of Christmas

I call upon you, for you will answer me, O God;
    incline your ear to me; hear my words.
Wondrously show your steadfast love,
    O Savior of those who seek refuge
    from their adversaries at your right hand.

Keep me as the apple of your eye;
    hide me in the shadow of your wings,
from the wicked who do me violence,
    my deadly enemies who surround me.

They close their hearts to pity;
    with their mouths they speak arrogantly.
They have now surrounded our steps;
    they set their eyes to cast us to the ground.
He is like a lion eager to tear,
    as a young lion lurking in ambush.

Arise, O Lord! Confront him, subdue him!
    Deliver my soul from the wicked by your sword,
from men by your hand, O Lord,
    from men of the world whose portion is in this life.
~ Psalm 17:6-14

Are we fighting our own battles? Are we trying to solve our own problems? Are we striving to be independent, to stand on our own two feet? King David was a warrior, a strong military leader, yet he called on the Lord to save him from his enemies. He didn't depend on the might of his soldiers, the strength of his horses, the qualities of his weapons. Instead he relied on God. He used soldiers, horses, and weapons as tools, but he trusted in the Lord for victory.

Almighty God, how often do we think we need to be strong to take care of ourselves. Instead, You want us to trust in You, not ourselves. You want us to admit our weaknesses and lean on Your strength. I am weak, Lord. I cannot defend myself from earthly enemies or the Enemy — Satan, the serpent, the devil. I will lean on You rather than myself, and when I forget and start trying to do it myself, remind me and turn me back to You. In the name of my Lord and Savior, Jesus Christ. Amen.

The Eleventh Day of Christmas

"If you love me, you will keep my commandments. And I will ask the Father, and he will give you another Helper, to be with you forever, even the Spirit of truth, whom the world cannot receive, because it neither sees him nor knows him. You know him, for he dwells with you and will be in you.

"I will not leave you as orphans; I will come to you. Yet a little while and the world will see me no more, but you will see me. Because I live, you also will live. In that day you will know that I am in my Father, and you in me, and I in you. Whoever has my commandments and keeps them, he it is who loves me. And he who loves me will be loved by my Father, and I will love him and manifest myself to him."
~ John 14:15-21

Sounds like a pretty simple equation: if we love Jesus, we will keep His commandments. But none of us can live up to that. We all break commandments every day, but we have the power of the Holy Spirit indwelling us. We must listen for the still, small voice and pay attention to it. He will lead us the right way, and He will reveal the Father and the Son to us.

Thank You, Lord God, for the Holy Spirit within us. Open the eyes and ears of our hearts to hear His voice and to see the path in which He leads us. In Jesus's name. Amen.

The Twelfth Day of Christmas (Eve of the Epiphany)

"For I know their works and their thoughts, and the time is coming to gather all nations and tongues. And they shall come and shall see my glory, and I will set a sign among them. And from them I will send survivors to the nations, to Tarshish, Pul, and Lud, who draw the bow, to Tubal and Javan, to the coastlands far away, that have not heard my fame or seen my glory. And they shall declare my glory among the nations. And they shall bring all your brothers from all the nations as an offering to the Lord, on horses and in chariots and in litters and on mules and on dromedaries, to my holy mountain Jerusalem, says the Lord, just as the Israelites bring their grain offering in a clean vessel to the house of the Lord. And some of them also I will take for priests and for Levites, says the Lord.

"For as the new heavens and the new earth
   that I make
shall remain before me, says the Lord,
   so shall your offspring and your name remain.
From new moon to new moon,

and from Sabbath to Sabbath,
all flesh shall come to worship before me,
declares the Lord." ~ Isaiah 66:18-23

When Jesus returns, everyone will recognize His deity.
Everyone will bow before Him. But it will be too late for
those who waited. We have to worship Him before His
return in order to share in glory with Him. We have to
choose to serve Him rather than wait until we don't have
a choice.

*Father God, I am eager to bow my knee to Jesus – not only at
the end of time when He returns in glory, but also today and
every day. I offer my worship and praise, yet I can never give
You what You deserve. In the name of Jesus Christ, my Lord
and Savior. Amen.*

The Epiphany of Our Lord

Epiphany

Now after Jesus was born in Bethlehem
of Judea in the days of Herod the king,
behold, wise men from the east came
to Jerusalem, saying, "Where is he who
has been born king of the Jews? For we
saw his star when it rose and have
come to worship him." When Herod the king heard this, he
was troubled, and all Jerusalem with him; and assembling all
the chief priests and scribes of the people, he inquired of
them where the Christ was to be born. They told him, "In
Bethlehem of Judea, for so it is written by the prophet:

43

"'And you, O Bethlehem, in the land of Judah,
  are by no means least among the rulers of Judah;
for from you shall come a ruler
  who will shepherd my people Israel.'"

Then Herod summoned the wise men secretly and ascertained from them what time the star had appeared. And he sent them to Bethlehem, saying, "Go and search diligently for the child, and when you have found him, bring me word, that I too may come and worship him." After listening to the king, they went on their way. And behold, the star that they had seen when it rose went before them until it came to rest over the place where the child was. When they saw the star, they rejoiced exceedingly with great joy. And going into the house, they saw the child with Mary his mother, and they fell down and worshiped him. Then, opening their treasures, they offered him gifts, gold and frankincense and myrrh. And being warned in a dream not to return to Herod, they departed to their own country by another way. ~ Matthew 2:1-12

The Epiphany is a significant event for us Gentiles. The Wise Men or Magi came from the East, following a bright star that led them to Baby Jesus. Unlike the shepherds, who were among the lowliest of people in Israel, the Magi were apparently wise, wealthy, and powerful. Most important, they weren't Jews. They hadn't grown up hearing stories of the coming Messiah. They weren't expecting a King—certainly not one in an insignificant foreign country. The Jews were God's Chosen People, but by leading the Wise Men to the Baby Jesus, God was showing that He loves all His children. Everyone can be saved. All are subject to the Lordship of Father, Son, and Holy Ghost.

Lord God, thank You for including Gentiles in Your plan of salvation. I am so grateful that You love each one of us and want us to come to a saving faith. I am thankful that I have that saving faith, that Jesus is my Lord and Savior. Thank You for all the blessings You bestow on all of us and give us grateful hearts. In the name of Jesus Christ, who lives and reigns with You and the Holy Spirit, now and forever. Amen.

Other Devotionals by Lillie Ammann

Finding God in the Everyday

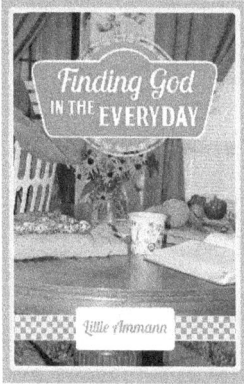

We expect to find God in church and in our private devotions. But do you wonder where He is the rest of the time—especially when things go wrong? With humor and poignancy, Lillie shares in ninety devotionals how she finds God in everyday experiences. "Welcome to the life of knowing God in the miraculous, other-worldly, plain ol' everyday." ~ Fr. Jerry Sherbourne

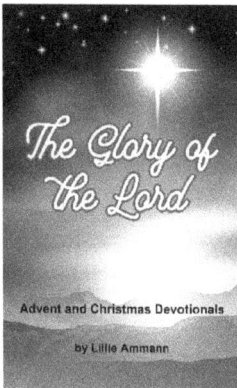

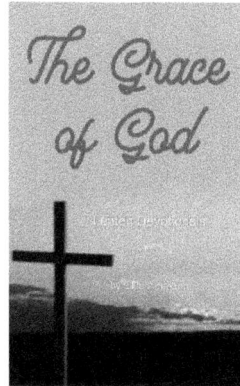

Time set aside daily for prayer, Scripture reading, and meditating on God's Word will enrich your spiritual preparation for Christmas during Advent and for Easter during Lent. The profits from the sale of these books are donated to Love for the Least.